Morning Star

Morning Star

Poems by
Margaret Holley

Copper Beech Press

Acknowledgment is gratefully made to the editors of the magazines in which some of these poems first appeared: *The American Scholar* ("The Perfect Transparency of the Artist," "Weeping Cherries"), *Beloit Poetry Journal* ("The Blinds"), *The Kenyon Review* ("Spinoza's Gold"), *The Laurel Review* ("Appleflesh, This Lily," "The Fireflies," "Peepers"), *Michigan Quarterly Review* ("Trash"), *The Nation* ("The Prayer Plant"), *Poem* ("Morning Star"), *Poetry* ("Eastering," "Koan," "The Tree of Life," "A Critique of Pure Reason"), *Prairie Schooner* ("Archetypes of the Collective Unconscious"), *Red Tree* ("Every Elizabeth"), *The Southern Review* ("Brahms' Requiem," "Half-Life"), *Verse* ("Blueberries") and *West Branch* ("Its Unfathomable Largo").

"The Mayflower" was originally published as a chapbook by the Bryn Mawr College Friends of the Library.

I would like to express my gratitude for the Seymour Adelman Poetry Award for support during the time in which some of these poems were written. — M.H.

Cover: *A Nocturne*, by John La Farge (1835-1910). Watercolor on paper, 8 3/16 x 7 in. Copyright © 1990 by The Metropolitan Museum of Art. Bequest of Miss Louise Velton, 1937.

For information, address the publisher:
        Copper Beech Press
        English Department
        Box 1852
        Brown University
        Providence, Rhode Island 02912

Library of Congress Cataloging-in-Publication Data
Holley, Margaret.
  Morning star: poems / by Margaret Holley. — 1st ed.
    p. cm.
  ISBN 0-914278-58-4 (pbk. : alk. paper) : $9.95
  I. Title.
  PS3558.O34964M6   1992
  811'.54 — dc20
                                   92-2577
                                         CIP

First Edition
Printed in the United States of America

for Andrea

Contents

I. Chorales

Weeping Cherries

Imported from the Orient,
seventeen weeping cherry trees
line the drive along the old summer hotel,
now a preparatory school for girls,

its turrets topped by the steeple
of the neighboring Presbyterian Church
where, in 1905, Bryn Mawr freshman
Miss Marianne Moore

of Carlisle, Pennsylvania,
entered her name in the registry.
Everything here comes from somewhere else,
it seems, even the voices

of the choir tonight
rehearsing Duruflé's *Requiem*
as if someone had opened a window in heaven;
even the mist, tasting of cumulus

blown in from the Carolinas,
drifting under the streetlamps, each droplet
bearing its seeds of dust and light;
even the long ribbons of water

making the woodflesh
open its mouths in flower,
magic out of A Thousand and One Nights,
the "singing tree" that Miss Moore

rightly called "a tree of knowledge"
grown up like the held and moving chord
of the moment; and even we, who live here now,
having risen from the dead

into such a world, with these weeping trees,
this black avenue silver with rain
and a grace never imagined
in quite this way before.

Six Harmonic Concertos

1. EASTERING

The trouble being that I can't hear myself think
any more. All the inaugurals of spring pass by
poised, forsythia bearing clumps of late snow,
pink cherry petals blizzarding under a blue sky.
We are hurtling in close again on the avenues
skirting the sun, causing the usual razzle-dazzle,
pinwheel narcissus, the green sweep of the willows.
I am so monumentally sleepy I must be made of stone.
I am an unraised slab on Easter Island, half-buried
in sweet brown mud and the memory of trees, sleeping
through sudden quiet into the eighteenth century,
waiting for Jacob Roggeven, still a boy in Holland,
to sail within sight and resurrect the mystery,
the lost heartbeat of all this cool volcanic rock
that once was liquid, a restless heart of flame,
before it was born into the blue and windy world.

2. KOAN

The sound of the St. John Passion before Bach
heard it. Rain at the windows, a pot on the stove,
the pendulum clock tapping softly on panes of air.
Cries of children, the flutter and cluck of geese.
Then wind whispering on the open road, running its
fingers through his hair, trumpeting up the halls
of the grand organ at Lübeck. What I hear is
your voice, making me feel loved in a new way,
and, in its silences, when I can be quiet enough,
the metronomic measure of these days soothing me
again, the furnace purring, sunlight brightening,
philodendron reaching from leaf to leaf — chorales
rehearsing in my lungs, a body gently at attention
in its daydream, flesh being made word again,
a child that is cherished growing up full of grace
and truth in the rough garden of the old self.

3. THE TREE OF LIFE

It's that time when grass begins growing its hair
long again, the little curled fists of leaf unfold
into sunshade, but Marjorie is not here to see it
except through your eyes, and my mother is still busy
in the Redding meadow, ash dissolving in rainwater,
drawn through narrow veinous halls into the trunk
and then straight up it — pure ascension in a dark body
a hundred years old, ashwater rising as sap in a well
of wood to the branching-out point, the variations
on a theme of open arms. Her death rose up through me
with unbearable bitterness, till I broke and broke
into leaf. All of my cells have died seven times,
seven trillion times, since I was just one of hers.
That's what the textbooks of embryology are all about,
division, complication, replacement of parts, the art
of outliving what intended us, hardly knowing how.

4. A CRITIQUE OF PURE REASON

What is one voice in the tidal wave of voices,
washing the city, so many solo instruments, all
of them sounding at once, uniqueness as spendthrift
as petals or snow, the commonest thing in the world?
Sometimes I can't hear anything but my own racket . . .
till something borderline, a cry of seabirds, a hiss
of waves, the verb embodied in the common noun,
calls me back to the saving chorus of otherness,
the peace of the mind when it comes to its senses.
Buds swollen, sonnets nearly ready to be delivered,
everything is held in the sway of its time — love
and work, work and love, the twining architecture
of sweet pea tendrils, and certain kinds of quietness,
Linnaeus at Uppsala probing the throat of a flower,
the privilege of absorption in the endless mystery
of simple things, all of them silent at once.

5. ITS UNFATHOMABLE LARGO

I know I'm awake again when the dream opens up
its own space inside me, about the size of an egg,
and the scene inside the little proscenium plays
again its brilliant baroque, never without mishap.
Too late — the six concertos have now been attributed
to Pergolesi, already dead at the age of twenty-six,
though they weren't his. It's all right — this isn't
mine either somehow. A life finds its own definitions
of error — yours, too, heavy with the unborn. I am
not yet writing this down, I am still speechless,
having to learn the peculiar shape of the patience
required by some words that are traveling toward me,
waves still far away in the inner sea of the ear.
All I can see is the rush of green, all I can hear
is the violin's body singing inside my own.

6. A REFINER'S FIRE

By the time the sky catches fire in a window pane,
the bright forges burning at the moving western edge
of night have already passed invisibly through us,
leaving a fervent goodbye to slide up windshields,
each eye a lake of tears lit flickering pink
by ether's smoking torches and the lace of trees.
Most of the time I simply can't see this being
never the same again, only how fast the hours fly,
not my own circumscribed notions of the possible
or how many kinds of night there might be waiting
— not the score of *The Messiah* written in 24 days
or years later, the composer, by then totally blind,
conducting a performance of it a week before he died
— only the grand auto-da-fé of another day's horizon
softening quickly to shadows and ash: the dream
of a dark driveway, the dark living room sonata,
the starry pillows of sleep and think, sleep and think.

Blueberries

The chipped willow-pattern china bowl
is older than she is, part of her mother's
set. Nothing is whole any more. What
matters is a gift of blueberries, the last
of the cream laced with their violet stain.

I know what it is she hears when she leans
toward the open kitchen door, a story
she has told me so many times: how she
as a girl goes out to find blueberries,
and the crows follow high overhead;

they watch from trees at the meadow's edge
as she wades into the bushes for fruit
plumped from green to purple to milky blue;
then they follow her home. The *cow-cow*
of the great black birds in the back yard

has grown fainter, words dissolve at times
into a pool of ink, and bruises appear
now like dark clouds in her skin, fading
from blue to purple to green, everything
seeming to fly backwards into infancy,

the gray haze of the back screen door.
The days become more and more like one
another, and more like a dream, the same
scene meal after meal — pagodas, islands
of awareness, a black silk feather blown

in from somewhere, a milk bottle rinsed
clear, dark fruit in the mouth, and a world
baked in blue, where two birds hover high
above the trees and three figures cross
the bridge — shepherd, farmer, fisherman.

I get up and take the dishes to the sink
with a new inkling of what memory is:
the bowl's invitation — *eat, empty me* —
the dinner plate's design come into view
and migrated from her life into mine.

Birdwing Bones

Anything can be broken;
   it's what holds
   and rises
I can't understand,

something in the hand
   as frail
   as dry leaves
and tough as living twigs

you cannot twist in two.
   The purse of skin
   splinted
by hollow bones, honeycombed,

with wind blowing through
   their catacombs,
   was able to fly
with all its strength

into a picture window of the sky.
   It slept on a branch.
   I remember
dreams of flight,

long arm bones rowing for height,
   and then the most gentle
   descent,
till I woke lying on my

shoulder, but now I am frightened
   by the blunt
   vestigial blades
showing through,

your skeleton, too,
   weighing no more
   than all its feathers together,
a useless

contraption for flight. Nevertheless
  your heart
  between two wings
pulses and flutters; what is

beyond you fills your eyes,
  looking
  and looking
for its own way to rise.

The Prayer Plant

dead, the boxes, bric-a-brac,
and her old bathrobe on the bed:
she has escaped at last its filthy
comfort, set us both unexpectedly
free.
      All this spring and summer,
driving Route 301 through rural
Maryland, slowly I begin to see

(as motion picture frames fool
the eye) in March, May, June,
July, out of snowy stubble and mud
the corn rising, *fructus ventris*,
its nimbus of gold seed grown
into amber haze over the fields,
and Jesus, her body gone to pieces
almost in my arms, the broken

bones — rib, shoulder, wrist,
four times one hip or the other,
and vertebrae — black eyes, dried
blood to sponge out of her hair.
"I love you," I whispered, meaning
you teach me (unwittingly) *caritas*
by meeting every gesture of it
with surprise and gratitude.

Like the white wafer of midday moon,
some things only seem to appear
out of nowhere,
               things so grave
and full of grace one could be
comforted, moved, torn open
even, to live on with such
invisibles in the blue sky.

Brahms' *Requiem*

Elisabeth Schwarzkopf calls it
"*Traurigkeit*" — "*Ihr habt nun Traurigkeit.*"
Is that what we have now, at eleven at night
with the lights extinguished
and ghosts of headlamps sliding around the walls?

In this concert hall of one,
what you hear is the rough lumber of limbs
being carved into the inner world of the cello,
the trumpet's gold searing black holes
in the chest, new chambers in the heart

as it labors to get its grip again
and again. In the words of Isaiah,
Psalms, Revelations, the Wisdom of Solomon,
you hear a man orchestrating his immortalities —
Clara Schumann, for whom he burned like a candle,

the dead man he loved, the mother
for whom his grief unleashed everything else
— and orchestrating ours, a helpless rebirthing
of ourselves within each other,
the dead being borne in the living,

this conjunction of dust — body of bone,
muscle, and blood already smelling of earth.
How could I have felt it too hard
to contain the "you" I loved and laughed with
after your flesh became "it," grass, empty rafters?

As you knew only too well,
it is not that grief is so beautiful,
but that only the borrowed voices of joy can bear
to rehearse, andante after andante,
its whole depth. Unexpectedly the notes

rise and spill over as ocean spray,
blown petals, parting of clouds, the returning rain,
silence ringing in the bones of the middle ear
and down that mysterious passageway
connecting them with the throat.

II. Inheritance

The Mayflower

One Indian climbs up to the summit
of what is not yet named Watson's Hill
and faces east into the wind off the bay,
the last man alive in his old world,

the first in the new. Pine woods, silver
in sunlight, watch over a beach of white
sand and oyster shells from which, six
years ago, he was captured and carried away

in the hold of Hunt's ship to be sold
for a slave in Spain. Escaping to England,
her traffic of ports, loading and unloading
knowledges, he lived for years in Mr. Cornhill

the merchant's house, sailed to New-foundland
four times in the fish- and fur-packed ships,
taught the traders how to set seeds in stony
soil, so like but not exactly his own.

England was a waking dream of everything
but home (he slept his unknown way there):
the gold crucifix of Spanish garrisons
borne through the smoke of Flemish cities,

war spreading out from Prague as swiftly
as couriers could run, and Captain John
Smith's amazing map of New England dotted
with singular trees and rocks, a spotted

wildcat, a church the height of its paw,
"the most remarqeable parts being named
by the high and mighty Prince Charles,"
the River Charles, London, Oxford, Plimoth,

and the horned head of a sea unicorn
snorting at Cape Elizabeth. When Dermer's
ship finally sailed him back into the harbor
of this hill, the home he had dreamed his way

back to, the shadow of that inked shoreline
finally came down for good over the summer
of his senses — beach, hawk, wind, water, sun.
The P for *Plimoth* was for his own Patuxet,

but he found the fields sown with his people's
bones, thousands, all of them fallen to plague
in his absence, unable to bury each other.
For days he slept and sat speechless among

their skulls, the bones lying on the ground
beside their dwellings and dry gardens.
Slowly he wandered into stories: Indian blood
spilled on English decks, reddening shoals

off Cape James, French blood on the sands
of Cape Codd, and English and Indian blood
mingling in the sands of Capawack and its
fictitious gold mine. At last he took to

climbing this hill to watch, an aging orphan
of all the lands he has left behind, his one
mind alone with them and their old and new
names: whales, no ships, wind, water, sun.

AT SEA

Memories now — blue heaven, a warm
wind's promise, silence on deck,
the canvas holding its breath full,
and all eyes watching astern, even

after the last shadow of England
sank into the indigo, sun-spangled sea.
And the anguish of leaving some behind
— Master and Mistress Bradford their

only son, Degory Priest his wife,
and others — none spoke a word of it.
"Sunday, September 10. All sails full.
Fifth day, first Sabbath at sea."

Then the sun hurried on beyond our bow,
beyond the lurid beaches of our dreams,
leaving us the ache of timbers, sickness
of many, and fear rising in nearly all

with a harvest moon the shade of sunset
steering us surely into the storms
of the equinox. And the last silence:
"Saturday, September 23. One seaman,"

a proud and very profane young man, who
cursed the passengers in their sickness,
telling them he hoped to cast half of them
overboard before their journey's end

and then to make merry with their things,
"having fallen sick with a most grievous
disease, died in a desperate manner."
Complete astonishment among the mariners.

"First death of the voyage. Burial at sea."
And now, O Lord, are we all to follow him,
for the pride and folly of this venture?
The waters gone putrid green and angry,

clouds dragging hairy bellies of rain,
drenching the deck, wind snuffing out
lanterns, our shouts and prayers alike
blasted away by the horns of the storm,

our bodies beaten against berthsides.
"Main beam midship bowed and cracked,
raised into place with the iron screw
brought out from Holland, then wedged

and bound. Much caulking of the decks
and upper works." Near half the seas
over now, blown out farthest beyond
any shore of human strength, we are

borne along, wretching and speechless,
on a Mercy as unfathomable as fierce,
the ship unable to carry a knot of sail,
pitching for days under bare poles,

helm lashed down, and all our cold bones
crowded into this catacomb between decks
with a wavering lamp and one spark in each
fearful eye of the living, divine fire.

AT ANCHOR

Mother-of-pearl, a milky sea,
a miracle — this morning of peace
sixty-seven days' gale from Plimoth
and twenty-one tossing in this cove.

Between two wildernesses, bruise-blue
water and a Jerusalem of sand and snow,
daily we pray for strength and cling
to every thread blown from beauty

over the rail of this ship, our home
— the moon afloat in a shoal of clouds,
sunrise shining in silver and silk —
more merciful than the stillness

of the land our heads swim over,
sea spray glazing in ice the heads
and shoulders of those pulling ashore
onto earth frozen a foot deep.

"Saturday, December 2. At anchor
in Cape Codd harbor. Whales playing
about the bow, one within musket-shot
but the first musket that fired at her

blew into pieces, both stock and barrel.
Peregrine, the infant born to Mistress
White this Monday past, is thriving."
Sabbath feast of mingled faith and dread,

a taste more salt than tears in every mouth.
"Monday, December 4. This day died
Edward Thompson, servant to Master White.
Burying party sent ashore after services."

Night watch over this nave of ice:
coughing in every berth, and the candles
of fever lighting the bowels of the ship.
We watch each other's faces flush and pale.

"Wednesday, December 6. This day died
Jasper Moore, a lad bound to Governor Carver.
Burying party sent ashore after services."
God of our Fathers, Haven, Shore,

House, and Hearth, now we begin planting
ourselves one by one in the soil of a new
life. Bless these bones, living and dead.
Bless this earth. "Thursday, December 7.

This day Mistress Dorothy Bradford, wife
of Master William Bradford, who is away
with the exploring party to westward,
fell overboard and was drowned."

After the shouts, after the billowed
sail of her skirt dove under a wave,
before the weeping — for one stunned
second of silence, a whole human world

at the railing studied the green water's
inscrutable designs of wind and winter.
Feathers of snow ride on the brine
so briefly before vanishing.

ASHORE

Creation re-created or undone? In this
new world of seas, dry land, and death,
we dig our bodies into the frozen clay
day after day long before seedtime —

Richard Britteridge, Solomon Prower,
Degory Priest — blades of the felling axes
hot, coals softening the stone-faced soil,
and flung sweat freezing into pearls.

"Tuesday, January 9. Plimoth Harbor.
Burying party ashore with the body
of Master Martin. The common house
nearly finished, wants only thatching."

Building and burial, fresh woodflesh
encloses us forever or burns and has to be
rebuilt. Smoke and ice, ashes and fever,
and wind prowling the face of the waters

where morning and evening the shallop
like Charon's carries the souls and goods
of our two cities. "Sunday, January 21.
First Sabbath services in the common house,

crowded with sickbeds." How small she
seems at sea now, our wet wood blossom,
her bell so distant and her mast trees
like double crosses naked under snow.

"Monday, January 29. This day died
Mistress Rose Standish." The roof
of the small sickhouse afire, seen
from the ship, burns like a spark

blown from the Indians' great fires.
"Wednesday, February 21. This day died
Master Mullens and Master White. Soon
there shall be but half of us alive."

There remain only seven sound persons
to tend the sick, to fetch them wood,
make them fires, feed them porridge,
to clean their beds and their foul

clothes. His armor lying an empty shell,
Captain Standish, bare to his elbows,
wrings the wet linen, hangs it to dry
by the fire, and rises in the night

to lift Master Bradford, near to death,
in his arms and hold the cup to his lips.
Of these, O Lord — the bag of rotted seeds,
the glinting ice in which we sow ourselves

— your spring will come, with or without
us, out of little winnowed down to less,
to gruel, faith, labor, and the thinnest
threads, the dream gold of corn silk,

sweet pea, mayflower pink, and the infants
born aboard her — Oceanus, Peregrine —
cradled, ark of our hopes, in prayer
and the holy ghost of each warm breath.

PLIMOTH, AUTUMN OF 1622

First we stole a cache of their buried
corn and a black ship's kettle; then we
took beans, more corn, baskets, pottery,
and they stole our tools — broad axes,

handsaws, and the long brush-scythe —
and several of Master Alden's few staves,
clapboard stacked for the return voyage.
Every shadow in the frozen forest had eyes

on us, as we hammered at the common house,
and the day we outlined our town site
the wind was flagged with cries and smoke.
Master Goodman and Peter Browne, lost

for two nights in the white maze of woods,
returned untouched, though never alone,
and Master Winslow with his man George Soule,
having buried Elizabeth, Ellen, and Elias,

kept our memory's map of unmarked graves,
that the savages might not count our dead.
Suddenly they appeared among us, tall,
straight, the two who knew some English,

and then their king, with his head oiled
and face painted a dark mulberry red,
white bone beads at his neck, some of his
men dressed in skins, others nearly naked,

and all of us visibly shaking with fear
as food and gifts went around from hand
to hand, translating our thefts into trade
in the common language of pomp and need.

It was Squanto who taught us to plant
fish in the cornhills, hundreds of fish
from a mere brook, to pull up sweet eels
from the beach of his ancestral land

with our bare hands, and who came to live
among us until he died in this month,
lonely remnant of the tribe of bones
native to the ground on which we have

raised our houses. Having burned away
with fever, his nose bleeding in streams,
he begged of Governor Bradford to be
permitted to enter the English heaven

instead of the Indian — a fitting trade,
since we have already inherited his earth,
our fields already cleared by his people,
the sweetest fresh water we have ever

tasted running in brooks and springs,
watercress, wild onions, walnut groves,
sassafras, sweetgum, strawberry vines,
and not only our own dead in the earth

that feeds us. In the year of our Lord
1622, by Francis Cooke for my son John,
who sailed with me in the first ship
at age ten years, and our posterity.

Spinoza's Gold

One thousand florins, the price of silence,
flared like a hearth fire and burned quickly
to cinders, the shame and safety of Israel.

Now he leaves through the streets of Amsterdam,
a seraph in common clay, God in the image
of Abraham having made an atheist of him,

a knife tip's script in blood on his neck
prodding him out of Egypt, its opulent ghetto,
its diamond trade and market for pictures,

past the house where Rabbi Manasseh ben Israel,
back from England's guarded doors, his heart
exactly as heavy as the corpse of his son,

barely lives to see his most brilliant pupil
banned and cursed in the darkened synagogue,
where his father's ghost already cringes

and black wax tears harden before the ark
of the covenant, scrolls of the law, the cry
of the shofar. Past the Breede Straat

where Rembrandt persists in spilling the gold
of this late July afternoon over blind Jacob
blessing Joseph's sons, Ephraim, Manasseh,

painting to please himself, they say stiffly,
creditors' letters piling up on the floor,
painting, in fact, from an older testament,

the human still life flooded with sunlight
and the dark mystery of love. Past bridge
after burning bridge over Amstel's silver water

and over the city's limit into the world
where every thing is a modification of God:
the silent faces behind him, the summer road's

untrammeled galaxies of dust, bees laboring,
the whole meadow humming, the nest hidden,
the seat of thought borne in its bowl of earth.

An Orphan Among the Mary Cassatts

Freud in his study
in Number 19 Berggasse
pondering his own dreams
and those of his children,
writing his way feverishly
into and out of the "family romance,"

Renoir at work on more
and more fleshy nudes,
Rodin modelling lovers,
and a Philadelphia woman,
living in France, sacrificing
motherhood to a career in painting:

Mother and Child.
Emmy and Her Child.
Margot Embracing Her Mother.
Simone with Her Mother in a Garden.
Mrs. H. O. Havemeyer
and Her Daughter Electra.

The artist who has
"found his subject," or hers,
embarks on a lifelong caress,
knowing full well in what sense
one can possess such things
and be possessed by them,

her theme repeated
in twos and threes — mother
and baby, mother and two children
— in the firm architecture
of furniture and arms, the touching
interplay of gaze and glance.

The observer, too,
drifting from room to room,
may have found a subject
and learned to move in pursuit of it,
luxuriating, turning need into memory,
filling in where necessary

the missing pictures
(Garden with Mother Gone
to Ash), learning, if art
has anything to say about it,
what heavens have been shown conclusively
to exist on earth, and in what sense,

and being seized
with pity — poor Margot,
poor Simone, to have to wake
one day from that beautiful dream
that costs you everything not to awaken from
and everything never to enjoy.

The Sleeper

At her head
the seven chimneys
of Detroit Ed-
ison release

their veils
into the light-
studded grail
of the city's night;

threads of fire
hum in the street-
lamps; and a siren's
aria retreats,

sailing downwind
to the river,
whose tarnished skin,
like tissue, shivers

under the moon.
At her feet
the hordes of corn
cut their milk teeth,

taking aim
at glittering skies,
where the phantom
jets exercise,

sporting in ozone
like swordfish through
waves of their own
thunder from here to

Kansas. Tableau:
the Detroit River
flowing like a narrow
vein of silver

through the city,
hauling its undertow
from Huron to Erie,
Ontario, the sea;

a man and a woman deep
in their troubles;
a six-year-old asleep
in the rubble

of their marriage; and
nineteen-fifty
now stained
with the spindrift

of another war.
Small bones
metabolizing fear,
her body tuned

to the steady
throb keeping time
at her throat, already
dreaming in rhyme,

she learns an alphabet
of things, rules
of grammar; the jets
tilt their jewels

over the pilgrim
waves; in the silence
of her dream
the dumb eloquence

of the depth of
those Great Lakes
begins to move
and tentatively takes

shape in words, but
she is thin passage
for the burden
of that tonnage.

Who will teach her
a vocabulary of
joy, some softer
constructions of love,

and where on
the homing flight can
she touch runway
and echo with human

voice the syllables
of that vast reach
of ocean — or is ours
its only speech?

Archetypes of the Collective Unconscious

Weaverbirds weave,
sew, and knot their nests tightly
   to the branch, knitting a long entry tube
below the main chamber.
   How do they
know how to do it?

   Even in captivity
a weaver's young — denied nesting
   materials for five generations and so
never having seen
   a nest or known a bird that had —
given twigs and grass,

   built a perfect home.
The sky gives birth each day
   to flocks of finches
who fly, mate, nest, sing —
   everyone talking at once, like us —
and die; daily

   the liver performs its
more than five hundred functions
   in the background, or the unnoticed
forefront, of that molecular
   symphony, the human
torso; and

   nightly the traveling
operatic theater of dreams
   plays in every language to its
rapt audience of one
   and all, never tiring of its
repertoire.

   I journeyed to Switzerland,
all over Europe, for twelve years
   and returned; I dreamed of being
swallowed by a crocodile
   and seeing inside it
walls of ancient stone.

"Little bird"
I called her without thinking,
   the lost child on the pier,
small thing in a nightgown
   standing out in the dark
hallway dreaming,

   sleepwalking along
the shore, eyes
   half-lidded in the ocean wind
— or was that a dream, too?
   You knew a mother's song
before I sang it;

   you know
who I am beyond all
   the details and incidentals
— you; you know the journey,
   the return, the sexual
union, the savior, the sacrifice;

   you know the ocean and why I finally
give you this "Lullaby" —
   Little bird, how weary you are
of watching the waves,
   and how long
I have been in coming.

Every Elizabeth

Gram said, "I named her that because
every Elizabeth I ever knew was beautiful.
And your mother was no exception."

A century ago Mrs. Stanton wrote,
"In my young days, when all life's problems
seemed inextricably tangled,

I often longed to meet some woman
who had sufficient confidence in herself
to hold an opinion in the face of opposition,

a woman who understood the deep significance
of life, to whom I could talk freely.
My longings were answered at last."

In some tribes every woman of a certain age
is considered the child's mother and every man
of a certain age the child's father.

And yesterday a friend wrote, "I have made
five new arrows for the hunt.
My kinfolk in the village sing to me."

Andrea, Travilla, Ruth, Nennette,
will the real mother of this girl please stand?
The whole crowd of ghosts rises.

Libby, you would be nearly a child again by now.
They mother you, too; they complete you;
listen, they let you rest in peace,

while I go on conversing through the chorus
of voices, their heirloom beauty
an inheritance I can only quote unknowingly

in gestures, wondering sometimes whose
are these hands, these words, and whose is this
love going through me on its way?

Siesta Key

For a minute I couldn't remember anything,
I was drunk on the smell of gardenias
lying open on their bush like handkerchiefs.

I saw my grandmother in the doorway, distracted,
holding a bowl of gardenias, so still
I could see her chest barely rise and fall.

I saw the empty beaches of Siesta Key,
dolphins wrinkling the green and silver tissue
of the Gulf, as it rolled its necklaces of shells

in to shore. I saw the sunrise-pink and yellow
conch mouths rocking in pools, and sand dollars
bleaching on the window sill. I even saw myself,

a ten-year-old hidden in the couch pillows
reading about Captain Horatio Hornblower,
her bones elongating in the sherry-colored shade.

I remembered that I had my grandmother's name.
I saw my mother very small inside her belly
and inside my baby mother all the cells

that would one day be her eggs. I saw us nested
like Russian dolls, one inside the other,
and time turning itself inside out,

seeds inside the buds in the bowl in her hands
in the breeze. I saw all of the people in the world
as one body, swelling and dividing in billions

of ways at once. I knew that we were living
forever in this room with its window open
like a womb mouth. And I saw my father

busy with the rigging along the boom,
with the mast beside him as tall as a steeple.
I saw the bougainvillea's red blooms

and its great mane of leaves smothering the fence
and my father hammering at the fence post.
Then I went back to sleep. I became

the blank page the story moves through,
filled with shouts and billows of warm wind,
with nothing left over but a foam of eggs hidden

in their salt pouch. No ships in sight,
just silky white water with a few spangles
and the endless rhythmic folding of the waves.

III. Firework

The Perfect Transparency of the Artist

Renoir at seventy-one
was lifted out of his wheelchair
to try to take a few steps:

"It takes all of my strength,"
he said. "I would much rather paint,"
and never walked again.

To his gnarled stump of a hand
he had the brush tied
and pulled its long hairs gently

through iridescent pools
of pigment and turpentine, turning
every reason to be bitter

and hate life — a stupid war
tearing into his sons' sweet bodies,
their mother, beloved Aline,

the girl with the puppy, gone,
and he, an old cripple and connoisseur
of pain, its knives

carving out every gesture
— into shimmering shapes, saying of this
condition, I am woman's flesh,

a child's face, I am peaches, water,
blue jewels of light, Venus, I am
love victorious.

Peepers

One amber inch
of blinking berry-eyed
amphibian,

four fetal fingers
on each hand,
a honey and mud-brown

pulse of appetite
surprised into stillness,
folded in a momentary lump

of flying bat-fish
ready to jump
full-tilt into anything

— the whole strength
of its struggling length
you can hold in your hand.

Its poetry, a raucous
refrain of pleasure
in the April-warm pools

of rain, the insistent
chorus of whistles
jingles through night woods,

Females! It's time!
that confident come-on
to a whole wet population

of embraces, eggs, tadpoles
— all head and tail,
mind darting in every direction

until the articulating torso,
Ovidian bag of bones,
results in the "mature adult":

a rumpled face in the mirror
still sleeping through Basho's
awakening plop,

re-enchanted daily
by the comforting slop
of burgeoning spring woods

and all this sexual chatter,
doing its best to make
the wet and silky season

last forever. Yet
as you lie dreaming mid-leap,
splayed in the sheets,

the future as a kind
but relentless scientist
feels around in your flesh

for the nerve of surprise;
he just loves
the look of wonder on your face,

the word on your open lips
for the immensity
that grips you,

Oh.

The Blinds

I remember sitting
with you one winter day,
you in bed sleeping,
you smoking in your gray

armchair, and I nearly
empty of everything I feel
or know now, looking intently
out into a veinwork, a snarl

of branches, our hands
and eyes behind the bars
of half-drawn venetian blinds
underlining the sky a dozen

times; and through it all, sun
-shine spilled over the sill,
bringing us at least one
more day. What I will

never forget, I am afraid,
with the trees turning their
bark to silver, the radiance
in my lap and in your hair,

the lines of light and shade
silently ruling the short
time left, is when you said
you never thought your

life was of much importance.
I was unable to explain my
speechlessness, then
as now, and certainly I

never dreamed I would devote
half a life's poetry to
showing you — can you see it
yet? Look at it through

my eyes now, each bit
of dust shining so brightly
for a moment as it
crosses the path of light.

Fugue

Black Iris by Georgia O'Keeffe
on the coffee table. Snow falling
    into the arms of the trees.
        A woman asleep on the couch.

White petals, or a landscape
of clouds and mountains in mist,
    like the snow descending
        past the darkening window.

Then the dark fur and frill
of iris, the O of an open mouth,
    a hole tunneling into
        the brown seam and ruffle.

Nothing is black or white here,
every pigment suffused
    with the faintest pink,
        flesh and blood's warmth

awash in the vast lockers
of winter and night. O stunning
    flowers, moon and starlight,
        city, desert, bones!

"I have one painting
and yards of failures dropped
    around me in bunches . . . so stupid
        I don't even destroy them."

Count nothing lost, no
thrashing, no stilted waste
    of an afternoon's blank page,
        no shifting figure and ground

of effort and rest:
the power of your dream
    is like the wind's muscles
        lifting pollen, voices, ash,

a blizzard of impulses
riding along in its restless arms,
and only the snow falling
perfectly every time.

Appleflesh, This Lily,

the fabulous onion, the edible tuliptwin
fleshing out a mystery of the self
itself, makes me imagine

every house I have lived in,
every man I have loved, in endpapers,
each story wrapped in its own silken skin

and bound together into one being, threads
digging down, the purple heart,
and the wild grasses waving overhead,

what Kant had the nerve to call
the transcendental unity of apperception,
the unknowable a priori integrity of all

that is you, a jeu d'esprit
of momentary madnesses, minute pearlfruits
plumping into a semblance of sanity.

Go ahead, Peer Gynt, peel away the parchment
and each successive layer to get at
the core; find at the center

nothing, only the aromatic oils
of memory rising from ruin; and still
this moonface waxing in black soil,

this suckling rootmouth, this wildlife,
this milky diamondwater meat of the metaphor,
quartered with a kitchen knife,

will make you weep, then feed you on
rain, on worm-softened earth
and the fragrant mineral sugars of stone.

The Violets

Out of East Africa
into the age of the antimacassar,
the mountain's round pubescent bloom — its androgyne
bearing into the drawing room a little jungle

of stamens hovering
around the ovary with Freudian attention
to detail and deep oblivion — having come this far,
internalizes by now all the fruitless verbs of motion,

everything being like it
that says *I grow, Make something of me.*
The leaves propagate freely in glasses of water,
raising their constellations anywhere light can reach

along the brownstone street,
shelved at sooty city windows among the spider
plants and philodendra and wonder that anything manages
to thrive here, that there is any more to breathe

than lust and dust-laden air.
Flowering in its pot, even in winter
bearing its one bloom, heart's tropic and hieroglyph
of the mind, the swelling stigmas' yellow silk

buds unrobe among the blue
petals like stars in twilight, divinations
of not quite domesticated hungers — Venus climbing
the evening sky with her high transport of knowledge,

winds that incessantly circle
the earth with word of it, and the repeated fall
of the sixty-second hexagram: Perseverance furthers.
Preponderance of the small.

The Fireflies

Sparks from a bonfire,
bits blown from a furnace,
they drift over the black meadow,

the pulsing shrimps
with their candles flaring,
each comma carrying its own lantern.

You remain indoors
reading by lamplight, glowworm,
larva whose labor is to eat, molt,

and feverishly expand
before the newly secreted
chitin hardens into another shell.

Out here it is a time of fire
between the first awareness
of desire

and its denouement,
a time of craving unfulfilled,
the bright transparency

of the verb "to want"
in all its conjugations.
For now, your cocoon of pages

keeps you as quiet
as the pupa, the doll,
that seems to just hang around

doing nothing,
while under the exoskeleton
a major transformation occurs.

What can I say to you,
except that out here sometimes
the body becomes an intermittent torch

finally consenting to burn,
consenting to know what it is
one wants

and may or may not have,
to walk in the dark by one's own light,
ablaze, transparent,

and as transient
as these, their minute lamps
making a silent firework of praise.

Chagall's *Violinist with the World Upside-Down*

By 1929 his world has undergone
    half a revolution,
and the whole town washed in red
    hangs upside-down,
Vitebsk stained with war, wrapped
    in Red Army flags,
dipping its roofs in the blue Dvina,
    a river of sky
bending westward toward the Baltic.
    Beside him
an upside-down pot of flowers
    hangs from an upside-
down tabletop by its own gravity,
    as if the inner eye
has caught an uninverted glimpse
    of things. To the silent
music of the latter-day Orpheus
    with clown-white face,
big ears, little hat, shoes planted
    squarely in the sky,
and small white bird on his knee,
    the lady Bella
floating angelic at his ear
    whispers endlessly
"Love, my love." He plays
    for her, partly
for joy, partly for ritual,
    partly for nostalgia,
the love of what no longer exists,
    except in memory,
that saves what still has value.
    Thus we bring heaven
and earth together in one frame:
    artists at work
on a background of what has vanished
    and yet will never
let go, the irretrievable past
    and its persistence,
Vitebsk in my heart, in my blood,
    my storybook.
I paint it because I cannot see it
    any other way.

Half-Life

The red stars of the cooling towers
burn quietly all night
over the waters of the Susquehanna,

and the last hours of March,
still bright with snow and black ice,
make forty-four years

ringing their changes down the halls
of my heart and brain. Once
in elementary school I wanted to know

about the nature of light.
What is it exactly? Waves of what?
Love like a phoenix

flaring again and again from ashes,
the X-ray's hot spot,
its coal nestled in the lungs' lace

like a valentine:
each one races to claim what it can,
the mind's candle wavers in their wind,

and the melting seasons
go on measuring rates of decay
in all the fictional units of time.

You are never asked to consent
when it goes out, the eye's bright treasure,
its second sight, compassion,

into the windy night,
and drags the rest of you along with it,
as quiet and surprising as the moonlight

that roams among the rags huddled in parks,
asleep in doorways, solitary rooms,
hospitals, prisons, everywhere

on this feverish god-earth,
bound up and turning in his balm of cloud,
burning helplessly at the core.

Trash

"To my knowledge," Ted Hughes reported
of Sylvia Plath, "she never scrapped any
of her poetic efforts." In the end

it was herself she threw, bright torment
that she was, while we move rather more
reluctantly toward an unknown finale,

each one dripping and dropping off debris,
involuntarily donating the body piecemeal
to the failing cause of its own renewal:

wet kleenex, sanitary napkins, towels
diapering blood, feces, the milky phlegms;
spit hitting the earth like a slap;

eyelashes, nail slivers, razor peppers,
and forty hairs a day, more or less, flying
off from each of us (where is it all?),

the invisible snow of old skin cells
landing on mirrors, lamps, and bookshelves;
in the twilight under the bed, a pollen

blooming into those angelic balls
adrift amid crumbs and crumpled letters
and the spiders' lace in the broom closet

and back hall, haloing the wastebasket
and waiting garbage bags, the cartons
of discarded books, broken furniture,

and bottle shards, even my love for
you, John Wallace, I still come home to
that wreckage, unable to throw it out

yet. The universal law of entropy
promises that everything will break down
into new forms of matter and conversely

matter to energy, flesh and bone, say,
into labors of love, hands moving across
clean sheets, even as the wind vacuums

wavering smoke from the crematoriums,
and gentle rain continues impartially
sorting and redistributing the dust.

For now I celebrate the slowest forms
of ruin: make me mulch for an unannounced
season, raw material for an untold story;

use me now, use me wholly up, before
tossing me back into the radiant furnace
of the sun's daily dancing artistry,

where everything and nothing is finally
transfigured, as each of us shall be
in that famous twinkling of an eye,

at that last trumpet I seem to habitually
sleep through, its gold and silver song
shimmering in the light of every dawn.

Morning Star

Hold Fast to What You Have Already
and I Will Give You the Morning Star.
Morris Graves,
from Revelations 2:25, 28

What we have is splendor,
clouded. We carry our own mist
like nebulous arms
enveloping lost beauties:
my mother's perfume invading the dusk,
elms greening the sunlight
down the nave of the Michigan street
where she disappeared,

dawn over New England hills,
cockle and ruddy and mother-of-pearl,
wonder beyond comprehension,
the cypress and lakes
of my years in the southern canton,
and my father's quietness,
a legacy rehearsed haltingly
till now.

Evening star, rising demurely over the ridge,
distilling day into one pure point
in the blue night,
morning star,
last flare of the dream world
to expire into daylight
and go on burning invisibly
and fall right on into rising again,

teach me to hold fast
to this letting go,
to believe in the unbidden wind
stirring and then leaving me
to burn gratefully
in the palm of hunger, desire, love
that grasps the world whole
in its open hand.